Starbucks Copycat Recipes

Prepare Starbucks Food and Drinks at Home

Copyright

Copyright 2019 New Wave Publishing. All rights reserved under International and Pan-American Copyright Conventions. No rights granted to reproduce this book or portions thereof in any form or manner whatsoever without the express written permission of the copyright owner(s).

Legal Notice

Content in this book is provided "As Is". The authors and publishers provide no guarantees regarding results of any advice or recommendations contained herein. Much of this book is based on personal experiences of the author(s) and anecdotal evidence. Although the author and publisher have made reasonable attempts to for accuracy in the content, they assume no responsibility for its veracity, or for any errors or omissions. Nothing in this book is intended to replace common sense, medical, legal or other professional advice. This book is meant only to be informative and entertaining. Encore Books and its authors shall not be liable in the event of incidental or consequential damages in connection with, or arising out of, the providing of the information offered herein.

Any trademarks, service marks, product names or named features are assumed to be the property of their respective owners, and are used herein for reference purposes only. This book was not prepared, approved, licensed, or endorsed by any of the owners of the trademarks or brand names referred to in this book. There is no implied endorsement for any products or services mentioned in this publication.

Get Free Recipe eBooks!
Cookbook Club

Fabulous Free eBook Cookbooks Every Week!

Our eBooks are FREE for the first few days publication. Be the first to know when new books are published. Our collection includes hundreds of books on topics including healthy foods, diets, food allergy alternatives, gourmet meals, desserts, and easy and inexpensive meals.

Join the mailing list at:
EncoreBookClub.com

Related Copycat Books
Copycat Candy Recipes
http://url80.com/copycatcandy
Homemade Copycat Liqueurs
http://url80.com/copycatliqueur
Copycat Appetizers, Vol. 1
http://url80.com/copycatapp1
Copycat Appetizers, Vol. 2
http://url80.com/copycatapp2
Copycat Olive Garden Recipes
http://url80.com/copycatolive
Copycat PF Chang's Recipes
http://url80.com/copycatpfchang
Copycat Dessert Recipes
http://url80.com/copycatdessert
Copycat Applebee's Recipes
http://url80.com/copycatapplebee
Copycat Panera Bread Recipes
http://url80.com/copycatpanera
Copycat TGI Friday's Recipes
http://url80.com/fridays

Contents

INTRODUCTION 1

Passion Iced Tea Lemonade 2
Mango Dragon Fruit Refresher 3
Iced Chai Latte for 4 3
Frozen Caramel Macchiato 4
S'mores Frappuccino 5
Chestnut Praline Frappuccino for 4 6
Mocha Frappuccino for 8 7
Ultra-Caramel Frappuccino 8
Salted Caramel Mocha Frappuccino for 2 9
Peppermint Mocha Frappuccino 10
Pumpkin Spice Latte 11
Café Vanilla Frappuccino 12
Strawberries & Crème Frappuccino 12
Caramel Brulée Crème 12
Chai Crème Frappuccino for 2 13
Cinnamon Roll Frappuccino 13
Double Chocolaty Chip Frappuccino for 2 13
Horchata Frappuccino 14
Java Chip Frappuccino 14
Matcha Green Tea Crème Frappuccino 14
Matcha Green Tea Frappuccino 15
Serious Strawberry Frappuccino 15
Strawberries & Cream Frappuccino 15
Vanilla Bean Crème Frappuccino 16
White Chocolate Mocha 16
Iced Lemon Pound Cake 17
Banana Bread 18
Vanilla Bean Scone 19
Pumpkin Scone 20
Coffee Cake 24
Cranberry Bliss Bars 22
Sous Vide Egg Bites: Bacon & Gruyere 25

Introduction

Tired of paying for expensive drinks and other food items at Starbucks? Yes, we love them too, but does it not feel like a pain to get up and pick one in the store. Not to mention all that traffic jam and crowd at the shop.

What if you can have your favorite item in a minute? Nope, we are not talking about some magic wand, but recipes just like those from Starbucks.

In this cookbook, you can find copycat recipes that look and taste just like those from the Starbucks. If you think there is a secret in making these, yes there is, but guess what, we have broken the code. Now, everyone, including you can enjoy delectable drink in the comfort of their own home.

Directions

The Directions for most recipes are very easy. Just place all but the topping ingredients into a blender and then blend on high until smooth. If it gets too think, add a little extra juice. A few recipes have different instructions which are included with the ingredients.

Passion Iced Tea Lemonade

Ingredients

- 2 tablespoons granulated sugar
- 1 cup prepared lemonade
- 1 Tazo Passion teabag
- Water
- Ice

Directions

1. Over moderate heat settings in a large pot, heat one cup of water until starts boiling.
2. Now, combine 2 tablespoons sugar with 1 tablespoon of water in a small sized microwave safe bowl & prepare the sugar syrup. Microwave the bowl on high for half a minute, uncovered. Stir well until the sugar dissolves completely; set aside.
3. Place the teabag in a large sized heat-proof glass & measure a cup of hot boiling water & then steep tea. Once the tea has steeped for 4 to 5 minutes, remove & discard the tea bag; set aside & let cool for 10 to 15 minutes at room temperature. Transfer lemonade and tea in a medium sized serving glass & top it with ice cubes. Add some teaspoons of sugar syrup; combine well with lemonade & iced brewed tea. Serve immediately.

Mango Dragon Fruit Refresher

Ingredients

- 1/2 cup of fresh red dragon fruit, cut into small pieces
- 2 cups of ice
- 4 ounces of mango juice
- 8 ounces white grape juice

Directions

1. Combine all the ingredients in a shaker. Shake everything together in order to break the dragon fruit, about 30 seconds.

Iced Chai Latte for 4

Ingredients

- 8 Chai tea bags
- Milk (to taste)
- 8 cups water

Directions

1. Over moderate heat settings in a large pot, boil the water & then add in the tea bags. Let seep for half an hour.
2. Remove the tea bags & before you add it to a pitcher; let it cool.
3. Let chill in a refrigerator or fridge for overnight.
4. Transfer half glass of the chai mix & top it with the milk.
5. Add in the ice cubes; stir several times. Serve & enjoy.

Frozen Caramel Macchiato

Prep Time: 15 minutes
Cooking Time: 5 minutes
Servings: 1

Ingredients

- 4 tablespoons whipped topping
- 1 cup whole milk, ice cold
- 2 fluid ounces original Starbucks whole bean espresso coffee or brewed Starbucks espresso
- 2-3 tablespoons buttery rich caramel syrup, thick
- 2 tablespoons vanilla syrup
- 8 ice cubes
- 2 tablespoons half & half

Directions

1. First brew the Starbucks espresso shot.
2. Now, fill a large glass with ice; leaving approximately 2 inches from the top; add in the whole milk and then pour 2 tablespoons of heavy cream or half & half.
3. Now add vanilla syrup & brewed Starbucks whole bean espresso on top of the milk.
4. Drizzle the indoor of your glass with thick caramel syrup & top with whipped cream; lastly drizzle a small amount of caramel syrup more over the top.

S'mores Frappuccino

Ingredients

- 2 tablespoons marshmallow fluff
- 1-2 tablespoons chocolate syrup
- 1 cup vanilla ice cream
- 1/2 cup milk
- ¼ cup cold coffee
- 2 tablespoons flavored s'mores syrup
- 1 cup ice
- 1 tablespoon whipped cream
- 1 graham cracker

Directions

1. In a large glass place two scoops of marshmallow fluff and top with some chocolate syrup.
2. In a blender mix ice, milk, ice cream, coffee and syrup until smooth. Pour in the glass.
3. Top with whipped cream and drizzle chocolate syrup and crushed graham crackers.
4. Note: replace ice with a frozen banana for an interesting change up.

Chestnut Praline Frappuccino for 4

Ingredients

Chestnut syrup:
- 2 baked chestnuts
- ½ cup brown sugar
- ¾ cup water
- ½ tablespoon vanilla paste

Praline crumble:
- ¼ cup pecan halves
- 2 tablespoons coconut sugar
- 2 tablespoons brown sugar
- 3 tablespoons water

Additional:
- ½ cup strong coffee
- ½ cup steamed milk
- Whipped cream, as desired

Directions

1. Make the syrup; Chop the chestnuts and place in a food processor.
2. Process until finely chopped.
3. Combine water and brown sugar in a saucepot.
4. Simmer the mixture over medium-high heat until the sugar is dissolved.
5. Let the syrup cool a bit and pour into a food processor.
6. Add vanilla paste and process until you have a smooth syrup.
7. Make the praline crumble; preheat oven to 350F.
8. Combine coconut sugar, brown sugar, and water in a saucepot. Bring to a simmer over medium-high heat.
9. Once the sugar is dissolved, add pecans. Spread the mixture over a baking sheet lined with parchment paper.
10. Bake in heated oven for 10 minutes. Place on a wire rack to cool down.
11. Transfer into a food processor and process until coarse.
12. Assemble; Add 1 tablespoon syrup in a glass. Add some coffee and steamed milk.
13. Top with whipped cream and decorate with pecan praline.
14. Serve.

Mocha Frappuccino for 8

Ingredients

- ¾ cup chocolate syrup
- 4 cups milk
- ¾ cup sugar
- 3 cups espresso coffee

For Topping:
- Chocolate syrup
- Whipped cream

Directions

1. Prepare the coffee as per the Directions provided by the manufacturer.
2. Mix hot coffee & sugar in a mixer until the sugar is completely dissolved, for a minute or two, on high settings.
3. Add chocolate syrup & milk; continue to mix for a minute more.
4. For easy storage, pour the mixture into a sealable container. Store in a refrigerator until ready to use.
5. Now, combine mix & ice (in equal proportion) in a blender & blend until smooth, on high settings & prepare the drink.
6. Pour the drink into separate glasses & top each glass first with the whipped cream & then drizzle chocolate syrup on the top.
7. Serve & enjoy!

Ultra-Caramel Frappuccino

Ingredients

- ½ cup skim milk
- ½ cup freshly brewed strong coffee
- 1 teaspoon vanilla extract
- Stevia drops, to taste
- 2 tablespoons caramel syrup
- 1 cup ice

Mocha cream:
- ½ cup heavy cream
- 2oz. white chocolate, melted and cooled
- 2 tablespoons freshly brewed strong coffee
- 2 tablespoons caramel syrup

Directions

1. Combine skim milk, coffee, vanilla, Stevia, caramel, and ice in a food blender.
2. Blend on high until smooth.
3. Make the mocha cream; beat heavy cream, chocolate, and coffee in a mixing bowl until soft peaks form.
4. Divide the coffee mixture two serving glasses.
5. Top with whipped mocha cream and finish off with caramel syrup.
6. Serve.

Salted Caramel Mocha Frappuccino for 2

Ingredients

- 2 cups skim milk
- ½ cup freshly brewed coffee
- ⅓ cup chocolate chips
- 2 tablespoons caramel mini chips or chopped caramel
- 2 tablespoons sugar
- 2 tablespoons whipped cream (topping)
- Caramel sauce (drizzle topping)
- Salt flakes (topping)

Directions

1. Combine skim milk, coffee, chocolate chips, caramel, and sugar in a saucepot.
2. Set over medium-high heat.
3. Simmer stirring until the caramel is completely melted.
4. Pour the mocha into the glass.
5. Top with whipped cream and drizzle with caramel sauce.
6. Sprinkle with a pinch of salt flakes and serve.

Peppermint Mocha Frappuccino

Ingredients

- ¼ cup water + 3 tablespoons
- ¼ cup brown sugar
- 10 drops peppermint extract
- ½ cup freshly brewed coffee
- 2 tablespoons raw cocoa powder
- 1 ½ cups warmed milk

Directions

1. Combine ¼ cup water and sugar in a saucepot.
2. Set over medium-high heat and bring to a simmer.
3. Simmer until the sugar is dissolved.
4. Add peppermint extract and continue to simmer for 20 minutes.
5. Remove from the heat.
6. Combine remaining water and cocoa powder in a heat-proof mug.
7. Add in the prepared peppermint syrup.
8. Pour over the coffee and milk.
9. Stir gently and serve. You can top with whipped cream.

Pumpkin Spice Latte

Ingredients

- 1 teaspoon vanilla simple syrup
- 1 cup coffee or 2 espresso shots
- 1 tablespoon pumpkin spice syrup
- 1 cup milk

For Garnish:
- Whipped cream
- Equal parts of pumpkin spice (ginger, cinnamon, ground clove, and nutmeg)

Directions

1. Add milk together with vanilla syrup & pumpkin spice syrup into a microwave safe jar attached with a lid or a mason jar. Seal & shake until the milk is double in volume & frothy. Remove the lid & microwave until the milk is steamed, for a minute or two.
2. Transfer the hot milk either into coffee or espresso & top it first with the whipped cream & then a pinch of pumpkin spice.

Café Vanilla Frappuccino

Ingredients

- ½ cup half-and-half
- 1 scoop vanilla bean ice cream
- ½ cup water
- 1 pinch vanilla bean powder
- 2 ice cubes
- 1 tablespoon whipped cream (topping)

Strawberries & Crème Frappuccino

Ingredients

- 2 tablespoon strawberry syrup
- ¼ cup vanilla ice cream
- 2 Strawberries, fresh
- 1/8 teaspoon Xanthan Gum
- ½ cup milk
- 1 cup ice
- Whipped cream for topping

Caramel Brulée Crème

Ingredients

- 1 cup strong brewed coffee cooled
- 2 cups ice
- 1 cup milk
- ⅓ cup caramel sauce
- 3 tablespoons sugar
- 1 tablespoon whipped cream (for topping)

Chai Crème Frappuccino for 2

Ingredients

- 2 cups freshly made homemade chai
- ½ cup coconut milk
- 1 ½ tablespoon vanilla-bourbon sugar
- 1 cup of ice cubes
- 2 tablespoons whipped cream (topping)
- Cinnamon powder, to sprinkle

Cinnamon Roll Frappuccino

Ingredients

- 1 scoop snickerdoodle ice cream
- ½ cup coconut milk
- 1 teaspoon vanilla extract
- ½ cup of ice cubes
- 1 tablespoon whipped cream (topping)
- Cinnamon powder (sprinkle)

Double Chocolaty Chip Frappuccino for 2

Ingredients

- 1 cup whole milk
- 2 tablespoons melted chocolate
- 1 tablespoon chocolate syrup
- ¼ cup mini chocolate chips, preferably dark chocolate
- 1 teaspoon vanilla paste or extract
- 2 cups ice cubes
- 2 tablespoons whipped cream (topping)

Horchata Frappuccino

Ingredients

- 1 cup whole milk
- 2 tablespoons cinnamon syrup
- 1 scoop vanilla sherbet
- 1 cup ice
- 1 tablespoon whipped cream (topping)
- 1 pinch cinnamon (sprinkle topping)

Java Chip Frappuccino

Ingredients

- 1 cup freshly brewed coffee
- 1 tablespoon chocolate syrup
- 1 tablespoon dark chocolate chips
- 1 cup crushed ice
- 1 tablespoon whipped cream (topping)
- Some chocolate shavings or chocolate syrup, for decoration (topping)

Matcha Green Tea Crème Frappuccino

Ingredients

- 1 cup whole milk
- 2 scoops vanilla bean ice cream
- 1 teaspoon premium grade Matcha tea
- 2 cups crushed ice
- 1 tablespoon raw honey or maple syrup
- 2 tablespoons whipped cream (topping)

Matcha Green Tea Frappuccino

Ingredients

- 1 cup almond milk
- ¾ cup organic pumpkin puree, no-sugar-added
- ½ cup freshly brewed strong coffee
- ¼ teaspoon vanilla extract
- 1 tablespoon raw honey
- 1 teaspoon pumpkin pie spice
- 1 cup crushed ice
- 1 pinch cinnamon (topping)

Serious Strawberry Frappuccino

Ingredients

- ½ cup pureed strawberries
- ¾ cup whole milk
- ¾ cup crushed ice
- 1 teaspoon vanilla extract
- 2 tablespoons raw honey
- ¼ cup whipped cream (topping)

Strawberries & Cream Frappuccino

Ingredients

- ½ cup skim milk
- 1 cup crushed ice
- 2 scoops vanilla sherbet
- 2 strawberries
- 1 tablespoon whipped cream (topping)
- 1 tablespoon strawberry syrup (drizzle topping)

Vanilla Bean Crème Frappuccino

Ingredients

- ½ cup milk
- 1 scoop vanilla bean ice cream
- ½ cup crushed ice
- ¼ teaspoon vanilla extract
- 1 tablespoon whipped cream (topping)

White Chocolate Mocha

Ingredients

- 3 tablespoons melted white chocolate (just melt in a microwave)
- 1 tablespoon instant coffee granules dissolved in 3 tablespoons hot water
- 1 cup whole milk
- 2 tablespoons whipped cream (topping)

Iced Lemon Pound Cake

Ingredients

For Cake:
- 6 tablespoons lemon juice, freshly squeezed
- 1 package lemon pudding mix, non-instant (4.3 ounce)
- 8 ounces sour cream
- 1 package yellow cake mix (18.25 ounce)
- ½ cup milk
- 4 eggs, large
- ½ cup vegetable oil

For Icing:
- 3 tablespoons lemon juice, freshly squeezed or more to taste
- 2 ½ cups confectioners' sugar

Directions

1. Lightly grease two loaf pans & preheat your oven to 350 F in advance.
2. Now, mix cake mix together with eggs, oil, pudding mix, sour cream, 6 tablespoons of the lemon juice, and milk in a stand mixer; beat for couple of minutes & then transfer the mixture into already prepared greased loaf pans.
3. Bake for 45 to 50 minutes, until a toothpick should come out clean. Before removing the cake from pans, let cool in the pans for couple of minutes & then transfer on a wire rack to completely cool.
4. Now, whisk the icing ingredients together in a medium sized bowl until smooth, for couple of minutes; evenly spoon the mixture over the loaves & let set for half an hour, before you slice them into pieces.

Banana Bread

Ingredients

- 3 ripe bananas, medium-large, mashed
- 1/3 cup chopped walnuts (in addition to 1/2 cup)
- 1 egg, large
- 2 cups flour
- ½ cup plus 1/3 cup walnuts, chopped
- 1 teaspoon baking soda
- ½ teaspoon vanilla extract
- 2 tablespoons buttermilk
- ½ cup vegetable oil
- 1 1/8 cups sugar
- ¼ teaspoon salt

Directions

1. Lightly grease a 9x5x3" loaf pan with the oil, dust with the flour & then preheat your oven to 325 F.
2. Blend baking soda together with flour & salt; set aside. Now, mix egg with vegetable oil & sugar until combined well.
3. Gradually add flour mixture to the egg mixture; blend well & then, add in the mashed bananas, vanilla & buttermilk; mix well. Fold approximately ½ cup of the chopped walnuts & transfer the batter into already prepared loaf pan.
4. Top the batter with the leftover walnuts. Bake until a toothpick comes out clean, for 50 to 60 minutes.

Vanilla Bean Scone

Ingredients

For Scones:
- ½ cup sugar
- 2 teaspoon vanilla extract
- ½ cup butter, cold, cubed
- 2 ½ cup all-purpose flour
- ½ cup heavy cream
- 1 tablespoon baking powder
- ½ vanilla bean, scraped
- 1 egg, large
- ¼ teaspoon salt

For Glaze:
- 6-7 tablespoon Heavy Cream
- ½ Vanilla Bean, scraped
- 1 teaspoon Vanilla Extract
- 3 cups powdered sugar
-

Directions

1. Line baking sheet either with parchment. Preheat oven to 400 F.
2. Combine flour together with baking powder, salt & sugar. Pulse in a food processor or whisk until evenly mixed.
3. Add butter & pulse in a food processor or cut in using a pastry cutter until the mixture looks like a cornmeal texture.
4. Whisk cream with egg, vanilla in a separate bowl.
5. Add liquid to the flour mixture & stir well using your hands until the dough forms a ball or pulse in a food processor until just combined.
6. Place dough onto a floured surface & briefly knead until the dough comes together; roll the dough out to approximately ½ inch thickness.
7. Make 8 squares & cut each diagonally. Cut 32 mini scones.
8. Place them onto already prepared large sized baking sheet & bake or until the edges start to get golden brown, for 10 to 12 minutes.
9. Transfer the cooked scones to a cooling rack & let completely cool.
10. In the meantime; whisk the glaze ingredients together in a large sized bowl, keep adding one tablespoon of the cream until you get your desired thickness. Dip the cooled scones in the glaze & then place them onto cooling rack again until harden.

Pumpkin Scone

Ingredients

For Scones:
- 2 cups all-purpose flour
- ½ teaspoon each ground cinnamon & ground nutmeg
- 3 tablespoons half & half
- 1 tablespoon baking powder
- ¼ teaspoon each ground cloves & ground ginger
- 1 egg, large
- 6 tablespoons butter, cold
- ½ cup pumpkin, canned
- 7 tablespoons sugar
- ½ teaspoon salt

For Powdered Sugar Glaze
- 2 tablespoons whole milk
- 1 cup plus 1 tablespoon powdered sugar

For Spiced Glaze
- 1 cup powdered sugar
- 3 tablespoons powdered sugar
- 2 tablespoons whole milk
- ¼ teaspoon ground cinnamon
- 1/8 teaspoon ground nutmeg
- 1 pinch of each ginger & ground cloves

Directions

To Prepare the Scones:

1. Lightly oil a large sized baking sheet lined with a parchment paper & preheat your oven to 425 F.
2. Now, in a large sized bowl; combine flour together with baking powder, spices, salt & sugar; mix well. Cut the butter into the dry ingredients using a fork, pastry knife, or a food processor, until no obvious chunks of the butter & the mixture is crumbly; set aside.
3. Whisk pumpkin together with egg & half and half in a separate medium sized bowl. Mix wet ingredients with the dry ingredients; fold well & shape the dough into a ball.
4. Pat the dough out onto a lightly floured surface & make a 1" thick rectangle (approximately 3 inches wide & 9 inches long). Make three equal portions from the dough by slicing it twice through the width, using a pizza cutter or a large knife. Cut the slices diagonally until you get 6 triangular slices of the dough. Place them onto already prepared baking sheet & bake until turn lightly brown, for 12 to 15 minutes. Place them on a wire rack and let completely cool.

For the Plain Glaze:

1. Mix 2 tablespoon of milk together with the powdered sugar; mix well until completely smooth.
2. When you can handle the scones easily, paint the plain glaze on top of each scone using a brush.

For the Spiced Icing:
1. Combine the entire spicing ingredient together & drizzle this thicker icing on top of each scone; leave the icing for an hour and let dry, before serving. Drizzle with a whisk using a squirt bottle.

Cranberry Bliss Bars

Prep Time: 10 minutes
Cooking Time: 2 hours & 35 minutes
Servings: 40

Ingredients

For Bars:
- ¾ cup white chocolate chips
- 2 sticks very soft butter (1 cup)
- ¾ cup dried cranberries (craisins)
- 3 eggs, large
- 2/3 cup to 1 cup brown sugar
- 2 cups all-purpose flour
- 1/3 cup granulated sugar
- 2 teaspoons vanilla or orange extract
- 1 ½ teaspoons baking powder
- 1 teaspoon ground ginger

For Topping:
- ½ teaspoon canola oil
- 1/3 cup white chocolate chips
- 1 -2 tablespoon orange rind, grated
- 1/3 cup chopped Craisins

For Frosting:
- 3 cups confectioners' sugar
- 1 teaspoon vanilla or orange extract
- 3 ounces softened cream cheese
- 2 tablespoons softened butter

Directions

1. Line in a 10x15" pan with the parchment paper & preheat your oven to 350 F.
2. Beat softened butter together with sugars using an electric mixer, until light, for 3 to 5 minutes; gently blend in the orange extract and eggs (don't overbeat the eggs). Add in the flour, ginger & baking powder; beat for a short time. Add in the chips & cranberries, keep stirring until just incorporated.
3. Spread the batter into the already prepared pan & bake until the edges turn light brown, for 20 to 22 minutes. Don't over bake the bars or else they would become dry. Let them completely cool.
4. Now, blend butter & cream cheese until fluffy. Add confectioners' sugar & orange extract; beat until frosting is fluffy & spreadable (if required, feel free to add 1 teaspoon of milk). Spread it evenly over the cooled bars.
5. Remove the rind from an orange using a zester; sprinkle the zest on top of the frosted bars. Coarsely chop approximately 1/3 cup of the Craisins & then sprinkle on top of the frosted bars.
6. Now, in a glass measuring cup; mix oil & white chocolate. Microwave for a minute until melted; stirring after every 15 seconds. Whisk or use a fork to drizzle the melted white chocolate across the bars.
7. Before slicing into pieces, let it rest for an hour and let the white chocolate to completely set.

Coffee Cake

Ingredients

For the Batter
- 2 cups all-purpose flour
- ½ cup granulated sugar
- 2 eggs, large
- 1 cup softened butter
- ¾ cup packed sugar, light brown
- 1 ½ teaspoons vanilla
- 1/3 cup half & half
- 1 teaspoon of baking powder
- ¼ teaspoon salt

For Topping:
- 1 cup packed sugar, light brown
- ½ cup chopped pecans
- 1 cup all-purpose flour
- ½ cup softened butter
- 1 teaspoon cinnamon

Directions

1. Preheat your oven to 325 F.
2. In a medium sized bowl; combine a cup of the flour with a stick of softened butter, brown sugar & 1 teaspoon of the cinnamon; mix well the mixture looks like moist sand. Add in half cup of pecans.
3. Now, using an electric mixer; cream 1 cup of butter together with ½ cup of granulated sugar & ¾ cup of light brown sugar until smooth & fluffy, in a large sized bowl. Add vanilla & eggs; mix well.
4. Combine flour together with baking powder & salt in a separate bowl. Combine the dry mixture with moist ingredients a small quantity at a time & then add in half & half; mix well.
5. Spoon the batter into a baking pan (9x13") lightly buttered & dusted with coating of flour.
6. Sprinkle the crumb topping on top of the batter. Ensure that the topping covers the batter completely.
7. Bake until the edges start to turn light brown, for 50 minutes. Let cool at room temperature & then slice into pieces.

Sous Vide Egg Bites: Bacon & Gruyere

Prep Time: 10 minutes
Cooking Time: 90 minutes
Servings: 6 pieces

Ingredients

- 3 strips of bacon cooked & crumbled
- 6 eggs
- 1/4 cup milk or cream
- 1/4 cup Monterey jack cheese
- 1/4 cup Gruyere cheese
- 6 4 oz mason jars

Directions

1. Set Sous Vide to 170 degrees.
2. Spray each mason jar with cooking spray.
3. Wisk eggs and milk.
4. Place bacon and gruyere cheese on the bottom of each mason jar.
5. Pour egg mixture in and top with Monterey jack cheese.
6. Seal the jars with lids and submerge in Sous Vide
7. Leave for 90 minutes.
8. Remove and serve warm. The egg bites can also be frozen and then microwaved for 1 minute.

Get Free Recipe eBooks!
Cookbook Club

Fabulous Free eBook Cookbooks Every Week!

Our eBooks are FREE for the first few days publication. Be the first to know when new books are published. Our collection includes hundreds of books on topics including healthy foods, diets, food allergy alternatives, gourmet meals, desserts, and easy and inexpensive meals.

Join the mailing list at:
EncoreBookClub.com

Related Copycat Books
Copycat Candy Recipes
http://url80.com/copycatcandy
Homemade Copycat Liqueurs
http://url80.com/copycatliqueur
Copycat Appetizers, Vol. 1
http://url80.com/copycatapp1
Copycat Appetizers, Vol. 2
http://url80.com/copycatapp2
Copycat Olive Garden Recipes
http://url80.com/copycatolive
Copycat PF Chang's Recipes
http://url80.com/copycatpfchang
Copycat Dessert Recipes
http://url80.com/copycatdessert
Copycat Applebee's Recipes
http://url80.com/copycatapplebee
Copycat Panera Bread Recipes
http://url80.com/copycatpanera
Copycat TGI Friday's Recipes
http://url80.com/fridays

Thank You for Your Purchase!

We know you have many choices when it comes to ready and recipe books. Your patronage is sincerely appreciated. If you would like to provide us feedback, go to http://url80.com/feedback.

Please Consider Writing an Amazon Review!

Happy with this book? If so, please consider writing a positive review. It helps others know it's a quality book and allows us to continue to promote our positive message. To write reviews, go to http://url80.com/reviews.

Thank You!

Made in the USA
Middletown, DE
08 December 2019